Oguz Konar

THE ULTIMATE GUIDE TO ONLINE MARKETING FOR SMALL BUSINESSES AND START-UPS

A 7-Step Blueprint to:

- ➤ *Attract New Clients, Customers or Patients*

- ➤ *Automate Your Marketing*

- ➤ *Dominate Your Niche In 60 Days or Less*

BY OGUZ KONAR

CEO of Local Marketing Stars

The Ultimate Guide to Online Marketing

Praise for *The Ultimate Guide to Online Marketing for Small Businesses and Start-Ups*

"The Ultimate Guide to Online Marketing for Small Businesses and Start-Ups is a must-read for maximizing marketing ROI. Jam-packed with powerful and proven strategies to attract leads, engage prospects and close sales, this book shows you how to take control of your online marketing and achieve significant and sustainable results."

-Pam Hendrickson

Best-selling author, Speaker, CEO of Content Solutions Group

"The Ultimate Guide to Online Marketing for Small Businesses and Start-Ups is a must read for all entrepreneurs. Chapter 2 on retargeting is worth 100x the investment of this book."

-Jimmy Nicholas of Jimmy Marketing and the Dan Kennedy 2013 Marketer of the Year

"In his book, "The Ultimate Guide to Online Marketing for Small Businesses and Start-Ups", Oguz Konar covers the most effective top-level marketing tactics you can use to get more clients from both online and offline marketing campaigns. The author doesn't just describe hot trends like retargeting (which he discusses in depth), but he also describes successful sequences for direct mailers (a time honored approach that has been around for decades).

So often, marketing books either focus on shiny new online tactics or tried-and-true offline strategies, but this book does a nice job of highlighting the best of both.

I recommend this book to anyone who wants to skip the fluff and get straight to "what's working now" to grow your business.

-Victoria Griggs

CEO, Straight Line Marketing

<u>ALSO BY OGUZ KONAR</u>

10 WAYS TO GROW YOUR PRACTICE IN THE NEW AGE OF MARKETING

THE CHIROPRACTOR MARKETING MACHINE

THE ULTIMATE DIRECT MAILING SYSTEM.

The future has many names. For the weak, it's unattainable.

For the fearful, it's unknown.

For the bold it's ideal.

__ VICTOR HUGO

ACKNOWLEDGEMENTS

To my forever supportive wife, Derya, who believed in me no matter what, even when she had no reason to do so at times. I am thankful and grateful for your trust and support. Couldn't have succeeded without you. Thank You!.

To my mother and father who taught me no dream is too small and believed in me no matter how ridiculous some of my dreams seemed. You taught me there is no other way to succeed other than hard work and an unshakable work ethic. I am forever grateful for your unconditional love and support. Your prayers made me the man I am today.

To my two beautiful sisters who taught me the sense of responsibility and accountability at an early age. It has been an amazing journey to watch both of you grow to be very strong women you two are today. It's assuring to know that I am backed up by two power house sisters.

To my mentors, coaches, friends and colleagues who have supported me during my journey of starting and building multiple businesses. Forgive me if I couldn't spend the time you much deserve with each of you. Thanks for unconditional support while I am going after my lifetime dream.

To the reader of this book, who may be just thinking about starting a business or maybe a savvy business person looking to add more ammo to your arsenal to grow and prosper your business. I hope that you have massive success in your pursuit and find the information in this book helpful to make your way to the very top.

Oguz Konar

TABLE OF CONTENTS

Oguz Konar

FOREWORD BY NOBBY KLEINMAN

It's been a long time since I first got involved on the internet. In fact, it was 1994.

So I have been around for a while and seen the many transitions from DOS based access to the latest Windows and Mac based applications.

Things are so much easier now than they were back then. Many who started when the internet first came out with dial up modems taking a horridly long time with that awful sound of the 'handshake' to connect would still complain today if the access isn't instantaneous at start up.

And then there is the software which abounds today as compared to earlier years. Originally, hard drives were around 20 mb (megabytes) because software was stored mainly on 5 1/4" floppy discs and the computer used mainly only to run the software. Terabytes of storage either on board or as back up is now the norm rather than the exception.

Of course, the whole industry is being pushed toward 'cloud storage' which is offered in in huge multiples by many providers. By way of back up and multiple accessibility it makes sense.

This book provides more than just basics to get anyone getting started and does so in a simple manner of easy to understand language without any jargon. It covers the other side of computers which is the business side - the money making side, the important side.

Anyone treading into the online space should read through the following pages and realize that unless your business world is one that lives every day in this space, then you are better off leaving it to experts. But what it does do is give a good basic knowledge and understanding of what should be considered.

It is a simple to read book covering many aspects spoken about by internet marketers and website developers. Anyone will get an understanding of what they need to know to enable them to enter into a meaningful discussion. It is not a bible of all the knowledge, but for those seeking to retain a modicum of control over their marketing, they will have a good foundation to start with.

I have many people who thought they could build their own websites or do their own marketing and advertising, only to find that their money has run through their fingers like water and never to be recovered.

Read the book. Get an understanding. And then consult people such as Oguz who can speak with authority because he has been there and done that. Experience is the best teacher. Learn from those who have trodden the path of mistakes before you make them yourself. Save yourself the heartache and lost money and time and instead seek counsel form those more wise.

But you can be well prepared. Just like interviewing anyone for a role or position in your life, prepare a document with all your questions, ideas thoughts and desired outcomes. Know in advance what it is you seek to have as a result. Are you promoting yourself? Your business? Or are you building a community or education site.

There's still so much to learn, and as the internet expands boundlessly, it is important to know your very direct target audience whom you are pursuing. Marketing direct to them and getting attention is desirable in order to generate profits. Again, all this is covered if even only superficially in these pages. But it's more than sufficient for the layperson to get an understanding.

An investment in education is a dollar well spent. This book is such an investment!

Nobby Kleinman - Dip FP BGB

CEO Money Rules and OutSource OK

INTRODUCTION

The problem most small businesses are facing today is; so many of them do not understand the vitality of having a well-planned marketing system for their business, although most understand the necessity of marketing.

However even those who search for tools, strategies and systems for marketing their business come across products and services that are designed for big corporations and billion dollar companies with unlimited marketing budgets.

What do they do?

They either spend their hard-earned money on various marketing activities and tools with little or no real strategy and "hope" that they would get a positive return on their investments or they begin developing the belief that "marketing doesn't work". Both are extremely dangerous for the longevity of any business.

That's the reason I felt obligated to put this book together to share with small business owners some of the tools and strategies, big corporations are taking advantage of, without breaking the bank.

The 7 Chapters in this book is filled with proven strategies and tools we use every single day to help our clients attract their ideal clients and grow their practice or small business at an exponential rate and get the best return on investment possible.

That's why I highly recommend that you take time to read and comprehend the tactics given in each chapter since they are the result of many years of hard work on identifying the most optimal way to maximize your marketing for small businesses.

Whether you only have an idea of a future business or you are already running a small business but struggling with attracting more and "paying" clients, or you might be in the process of expanding your business and looking for marketing strategies to automate your marketing, so you can focus on what you do best, which ever one is your situation, the tools covered in these chapters will give you the necessary ammo to add to your arsenal to make the most of your marketing dollars.

To your success....

Oguz KONAR

Serial Entrepreneur

Founder and CEO of Local Marketing Stars

Info@localmarketingstars.com

About Local Marketing Stars

Who we are?

Local Marketing Stars is the leading Marketing Agency in The Tri-State Area focusing on **helping small businesses, practices and start-ups grow and strategically increase their profits through designing and implementing effective marketing systems**.

The core of our marketing philosophy, which we use to help practices and small businesses, is Local Marketing Stars Marketing Success Formula.

Local Marketing Stars has been featured on major media channels, and received numerous awards for the quality of the work we do and the results we get for our clients consistently.

What we do?

Our Marketing Success Formula has been revolutionary to many businesses like you; We simply have three goals;

1.) Find the right market for your products and services

2.) Deliver the right message to your target audience
3.) Use all the right media tools to get your voice heard, attract clients and customer.

Our Services include:

- Social Media

- Search Engine Optimization (SEO)

- Local Search

- Web Design and re-Design

- Reputation Management

- Multi-Channel Marketing

- E-Mail Marketing

- Content Creation

- Video Marketing

- We also offer private consultation to limited number of clients.

When you are ready to talk more, call us from 8:30 AM EST to 5:30 PM EST at 917-746-0099 or apply for a <u>complimentary consultation</u> by e mailing us at

<u>info@localmarketingstars.com</u>

CHAPTER 1

WEBSITES

Build a Website Optimized for Conversion that's Mobile Friendly

The new trend for the future is that mobile traffic is going to surpass desktop Internet traffic even more than it is today. Your traffic conversion and search engine rankings depend upon having a website optimized for mobile devices as well as the conversion of traffic into leads and sales. The site may display on a mobile phone, but it might not be "mobile friendly."

The site has to fit onto a mobile screen so there's no scrolling or zooming involved and the content is easily viewable. The buttons and links have to be big enough to be tapped with a person's thumb. A site that is optimized for conversion makes it easy for your users to find information that's important to them. One touch directions and tap to call are some of the most useful features that you'll want to have.

Other options include email signup forms, scheduling options, and mobile coupons to help with the conversion rate of your site. Your site also needs social media links as well as videos which are now very popular ways of accessing your content. You need a dedicated mobile site and one that's responsive.

Each site has its advantages which you can apt to use to get the best results.

Why Do I need a mobile Website?

We live in the digital age so a website is essential. You may be one of these people that come from word of mouth referrals, but the statistics don't lie. It's estimated that about 67 % of men and women use the Internet first to find information about a business or to just search to try and find one.

Last year, when I needed a new CPA. I talked to a friend of mine about my need. And he gave me the names of two individuals. I have found the potential solutions to what I was looking for. I turned to Google first thing and typed in the name of the first referral.

The results were dated and the website was hard to navigate. I thought that because he was a CPA he might not have a lot of knowledge about marketing and digital media. I went down the list and looked at the LinkedIn profile which wasn't setup correctly. There was no experience, education or a decent photograph listed which started to worry me. The third on the list was his Yelp reviews and he had two stars out of five and poor feedback. I called my fried and had a discussion about his judgment.

I then called the second name I had in my list and found out that he had a nicer site, but it wasn't that modern. There wasn't any negative reviews and he had decent email account that wasn't some free site like Yahoo. If you want more media exposure, then you need a law site that's user-friendly.

When a potential customer begins research, the often begin online. They look for a talking head, a quote, or experts in a certain field of work. They are looking for the best option. Which in today's world is an attractive well laid out website.

E-mail Addresses

An email address should not be neglected. You want one that is professional such as name@thisfirm.com, not greatattorney@gmail.com. The first one is the option that you want. You should have an address that is linked to your company website domain name or your expertise in general.

If you were a plumber in New York for example, a good SEO website would be bestplumbernewyork.com or something along those lines and people could remember that.

"Mobile Friendly" Design

Once a website has been developed, you need a mobile friendly site and a one that's responsively designed. There are over 1.2 billion people using smartphones to access the Internet. If you don't have a mobile website then you're not going to get as much business and you'll end up losing money as a result. You want people to visit your website on all platforms and find all your information with ease.

Avoiding Simple Webdesign Mistakes that are costing you clients today.

Many websites suffer from some of the most common mistakes which can drastically affect their efficiency. Most of these can be easily prevented. A number of these problems just lead to annoyance; others restrict or bar people visiting your site from gaining access to the content or functionality which is essential for conversion.

Despite how nicely or inadequately your site is set up, mostly, the biggest mistakes happen when the website's purpose in the general plan of your business has not been considered in detail.

It is only when the purpose of your site is identified and work of the site are comprehended, that the site is able to be set up in a way which attains these goals. For example; in the case of a pilot, this is similar to maneuvering your plane for a lovely, smooth landing, just to realize that you landed at the inappropriate airport.

We have collected a list of 17 common errors with useful tips on how to keep away from them. We hope that this list is going to assist you to make sure that your site is not affected in a similar manner.

1. **Lack of Accessibility;**
   Accessibility means how easily a huge number of users can visit your site. On a certain level, it can connect to the specific web browsers which are utilized

by individuals with a deformity; an important market by their own standards. It also indicates the wide range of equipment, browsers and functional systems which are utilized for surfing the web. Some examples to think about are:

Individuals who are visually impaired also surf; does your site's font become bigger if a visitor alters the size of text in their browser from 'medium' to largest?' Does your site's page layout become distorted when a visitor alters the text size?

Small objects: How does your site appear when accessed from a cell phone or IPad? How long does it take the load the page?

Different Operating Systems: Internet Explorer from Microsoft does not operate on Mac or Linux. What is the appearance of your website design on Safari, FireFox or Opera?

Ancient Browsers: Unbelievably, there are still a lot of users operating browsers which are 4 or 5 years old without any update. A great website designer will make use of the latest browsers' ability to format and present, and at the same time 'politely degrading' when watched with an ancient version.

Screen Sizes: A large production of different screen sizes has occurred. Your site should have the ability to display properly on screens of various sizes: It should not be taken for granted that the user is going to have their entire screen assigned to their browser.

2. **Infrequently asked questions;**
    Have you studied a FAQ page and been annoyed by the unimportance of the queries? Have you asked yourself if the queries had ever been presented, leave alone often? If yes, then you are not the only one. A lot of sites do not have FAQ pages anymore; rather, they have enhanced their content to give this

information. But, the lesson here is not mainly about how stylish the FAQ is or not; the lesson is that all your site's content should be important to the individuals who will possibly visit the site. Important content will offer them a great image and will raise the possibility that they will venture further and turn into a client.

3. **No contact information/Or can't find it**

   We are continuously fascinated by sites which make it hard to get information on physical contact. For companies which are small or medium, this is serious, as your information on contact offers an important connection to reality, assuring clients they are working with a genuine business and not a con. Contact data should be inclusive of traditional contact techniques like phone and the address of your business.

4. **Click here to "Enter"**

   Do not squander your visitor's time with a site for 'click here to enter' link or a flashy splash screen. A visitor to your website is present already; therefore, appreciate them instantly, with helpful, important content.

5. **Use of Audio**

   Use of audio should be kept to a minimum on any website and at no time should it be played repeatedly, particularly if you are attempting to communicate with users in a business setting. The ideal sites which utilize audio need the user to click on an icon for 'play.' For sites which require a voiceover, you will drastically improve your company's impression by ensuring the track is recorded expertly.

6. **Too much flash**

   Flash is ideal when utilized at a minimum and stylishly. Flash can provide vibrancy and motion to your site; providing abilities which are hard or impossible, by just utilizing HTML. Sadly, it has two main disadvantages; not every person has flash or the bandwidth to back flash. If you have made up your mind that it is right to utilize a large flash element on your site, you should ensure then, that the user gets visual feedback as it loads.

7. **Meaningless Graphics**
Your site's pictures should improve user experience. A balance should be struck on this; sufficient to facilitate the site's beauty and function, but not sufficient to form clutter and make the user experience slow. Site pictures should be optimized to make sure that the site is portrayed at a speed which is reasonable.

8. **Search Engine Unfriendliness**
Having a site which has an easy to use search engine does not promise you top rankings on your preferred search engine (this technique is known as Search Engine Optimization). There is no good reason for not having carried out the basics. These are: Possessing a site map, precise and important content, utilizing normal mark-up tags which are acknowledged by search engines and meta tags also, like keywords and an illustration.

9. **Welcome to Our Site**

   Start your content with material which is a bit more attractive than 'Welcome to our website.' An opening like this seems childish and tells the visitor that the site is not in a hurry to give them helpful information.

10. **Navigation Challenges**

    Moving around your site ought to be instinctive. This means that the site navigation should be well arranged and provided in a method which complies with recognized web navigation regulations. Adhere to normal methods and normal sites for navigation factors like menus and links. Links should appear like links.

    A visitor should have easy access to links such as 'home' and 'contact us.' Apart from having navigation factors which are easily identifiable, it is vital to consider the logical arrangement of your site. One helpful metric to remember is the average number of clicks required to get some information or to have access to a page. Another main factor is how simple or obvious it is for a visitor to discover the link to click on. For instance, to locate 'two sided tape' on your site, should they search under 'Office Supplies' or Art & Craft?'

11. **Flawed Color Schemes**

A color scheme which is poor will make visitors deviate from your message. Worst of all, the message is going to be illegible. It is vital as well to remember users who are visually impaired; therefore, if your site has colored content and the background is colored, it would be advisable then, to provide an option of high contrast. This can be carried out easily by making use of style sheets.

12. **Don't expect visitor to read entire webpage**

A minimum number of people read the entire webpage. Instead, people skim web pages searching for important information, zeroing in on the factors which attract them. Therefore, it is vital to arrange information well and ensure it is simple to get on the page.

13. **Pop-up Madness**

Avoid pop-up windows unless you possess an extremely valid reason. They are annoying and a lot of browsers ban them.

14. **Dead Links**

Each of the links of your site should function. It will seem unprofessional if users come to your site and find broken links. It will lead to frustration and your visitors' confidence in your site, and hence your company, will decrease. Each link on your site ought to be tested appropriately. Links to outside sites which you do not control need to be tested regularly, particularly if they link deep into that site's content.

15. **Don't ask visitors to install a software**

In general, users are not going to be keen on installing software to view your site's content. By default, a lot of browsers restrict websites from setting up software. Extensions or applications like Acrobat and Flash are excluded from this rule and have achieved acceptance widely.

16. Too slow to load

Web surfers are known to be impatient and punish sites which are slow by leaving them. A great site loads in just a few seconds. Factors which lead to pages loading slowly are burdening a site with meaningless pictures, sub-optimal picture formats and having factors like utilizing an international hosting firm or a 'backyard' hosting firm. If a genuine and unavoidable reason exists for experiencing a slow site, then give the visitor visual feedback as it loads.

17. Not Keeping an eye on your site

A number of tools exist to supervise your site. They can offer useful details on the trends of your users on your site, enabling you to know their origins, ways they used to discover your site, what type of content interests them, and the links which are most famous.

With wonderful tools available, at no charge, there is not reason for not monitoring who visits your site and what they engage in after arrival.

> Contact our marketing team to have a FREE analysis of your website to find out if you are making the mistakes outlined here and receive a strategy session on how to fix them.

CHAPTER 2

The practice of serving ads based on prior engagement is what we call retargeting. There are many forms of this technology, but the most common one is site-based retargeting. There's also Facebook retargeting, mail retargeting, CRM retargeting as well as others.

When you use site-based retargeting, you serve ads to people that leave your website. The retargeting showcases your brand on other sites on the web that the visitor goes to and this keeps your brand in their mind in an attempt to bring them back to the site. A cookie stores the site visit, but not any sensitive information.

Understanding Site Retargeting

Cookies are used during site retargeting. When you get a site visitor, there's a few lines of code given to the retargeter and this is dropped via an anonymous browser cookie. This cookie is a small file with information on it. There's no sensitive information stored on the cookie just the site visit. When the person leaves your site the cookie tells the retargeter when that bounced person is on another site. If there's ad space on that site, the retargeter bids on that space in real-time or RTB bidding and if they are the high bidder the ad is secured before the page even loads. This process ss automated and takes less that a second to complete. Once the page loads, the ad space is already purchased and the ad for your website will appear with the page content. Many e-commerce companies use retargeting as it's an effective way to get bounced traffic back to your website and shopping again.

Many companies besides just e-commerce ones can benefit from retargeting. Many B2B companies are often the perfect candidates for retargeting, as it helps them stay in front of their leads. Schools can use retargeting for donations, or to increase their enrollment. To keep companies in front of qualified applicants, recruiters often use retargeting too. Merchandise sales or tickets are often purchased more often when Events or entertainment brands use retargeting. There are many ways to apply retargeting and if you're not getting 100% conversion rates then you can use retargeting effectively.

How can Retargeting help small businesses?

Direct Response and Branding

Direct response campaigns are often associated with retargeting. To provide a timely deal to consumers or to get people to "Click Now," banner advertisements are often used. When a visitor goes to your site or has engagement with your brand, but then leaves without a conversion taking place, you have an opportunity to get that person to come back to your site when you use retargeting.

The retargeting campaign and advertising you choose you can send them relevant messages. For example, if a person left a shopping cart after the shipping costs were calculated, you can send them offers such as free shipping for 24 hours to entice them back to buy from you.

This sort of digital advertising is more than just getting click to your website. You can create campaigns to showcase your brand, get demographic information, past purchase information, search history, and so on, which can help to create effective brand campaigns. Most of your return visits will come through search. One study showed a 1046 percent increase in branded search when a retargeting campaign was used. This huge increase is a big indicator that rebranding is very successful when it comes to building a brands awareness and it just isn't for direct response campaigns.

Creatives for Retargeting

One of the cornerstones of any online display campaign is banner design. When you have a good banner ad you have concise messaging due to the simple banner design which showcases your message clearly.

When you want to have more brand awareness, a good slogan and logo with the fonts and colors of your company are easy to incorporate into the advertisement. Some tips to create killer banner ads are:

Avoid Distractions

You want to avoid having too much in your banner advertisements. This really won't help you much because it ends up confusing people more than actually helping them and they will miss the meaningful information you wish to convey. You only have a moment with any banner ad to capture the attention of the person viewing the advertisement.

You also only have a small space on a webpage for your banner ad, so you have to make the best use out of this space. You don't want too much text or complicated graphics to crowd out the small space that you have to work with.

You want to make a lasting impression with the advertisement. You need short taglines and backgrounds that catch the eye of the viewer. Taglines should explain your products or services clearly to the viewer. The call-to-action should be declarative, bold and simple.

A photograph with a person can work, but sometimes this can backfire. If you add these in with no clear goal, then they aren't going to work in the way you want them to. You want to explain your product and often the photograph will be overlooked.

An advertisement with simple artwork and a bright colored background can be more beneficial to you. This makes the ad more eye-catching to the viewer. In some cases the photograph of a person can work for you. If the person is using the product you're selling in the advertisement then this is going to be better for you. This will depend on the advertisement itself and the room you have to work with. It may work and it may not.

If you use photographs, they need to show the benefit of your service or product like piece of mind or convenience. If you're able to somehow show the benefits of a service or product, then this is going to be very beneficial to you. Your bottom line is to have a readable, simple, and beautiful banner ad and don't have anything that takes away from that. You want to make sure you don't have over-complicated testing of the ad as well.

Can You Benefit From Retargeting?

Vibrant artwork and bright colors often work better than a photograph. To run a successful campaign, retargeting can help you. The following best practices will help you make the most out of retargeting for your advertisement to create your brand awareness and a return on your investment.

Retargeting Best Practices

1.) Frequency Caps

You need to be visible, but you don't want any overexposure. To accomplish this, the use of a frequency cap is your best option. If there's one or two visits to the website, this doesn't mean that your ads will be everywhere for the prospects. If there's overexposure then the performance of the campaign will be decreased.

You may find that prospects will ignore the advertisements altogether which we call banner blindness. They see your banner as an annoyance and it has a stalking-like effect on them. The frequency cam limits the number of times the tagged user sees the advertisement. This prevents the user from feeling overwhelmed, stalked, or bored by your ads.

You need to be strategic with how the ads are served. Potential prospects may still be window shopping, researching or just not in a mood to buy yet. Our typical recommendation is for about 17-20 ads per month for each user, but it's up to you to determine the level of your retargeting campaign.

2.) What is a 'burn code' and how to use it.

You may have purchased something online before and then been swapped with advertisements from that product or company after you buy. If this is the case then the company doesn't see you as a current customer and the company is just annoying you.

You don't want to make this mistake and you can avoid it with what is called the burn pixel. This is a snippet of code that is placed on the post-transaction page. It un-tags anyone that makes a purchase which stops the serving of ads to them. This eliminates the annoyance to the customer and the burn code snippet will save you money.

You don't want to waste dollars and people that have already been converted and purchased from you. You can still make converted customers a part of the retargeting campaign, but they shouldn't have to make the same action twice.

You now have the opportunity to serve new ads to these customers not ones from what they have already bought. You want to cross-sell, upsell and maybe even offer referral discounts through new advertisements.

3.)Being Crystal Clear Segmenting Your Audience

When you use audience segmentation, you're tailoring the advertisement to users that are different stages of their purchase. You take retargeting pixels and put these on different pages of the site and then you tailor creatives which are based on the depth of engagement of the person on that page.

When the user comes to the main page, they can be targeted with creatives that help to create your brand awareness. If they are looking at product pages you can target them with product offerings.

With audience segmentation, you keep users engaged no matter their level of interest by serving them meaningful ads no matter where they are on your site.

4.)Use Geographic, Demographic, and Contextual Targeting

You can fine-tune advertisement placement by using targeting. This helps increase the performance of your ads and create greater relevancy too. You can use demographic information which is gender, and age, contextual factors like the subject matter on the website, or use geographic style data.

When you use contextual and demographic data you aren't wasting your valuable ad impressions on people that have no relevance to your campaign.

The targeting improves relevancy of the retargeting campaign as it gets the ads in front of the right people, but it also helps to lower your costs. You aren't showing ads to people who have no interest, you're getting the ads to the right people which increases the chances that you'll get a sale.

5.) Making the best use of 'conversion windows':

To establish market share and increase awareness brand markers can use display to create a measurable channel which is effective. The direct response crowd often has a complaint that online display advertising doesn't drive clicks the same way that paid search advertising does. The clicks aren't the whole story as retargeted ads can provide brand lift even if they aren't clicked. As mentioned before one study showed 1046% increase in branded search with retargeted ads which shows recall and brand awareness.

Some ads don't create an immediate buying decision but this can influence people to make a purchase at another time which we call the billboard effect. A billboard can attract a person and create brand awareness. This can be the same with an online display advertisement which can trigger an action later on by the viewer. .

View-through conversions can give advertisers rich data around their ad performance as they can see how soon a conversion occurs after a person views an advertisement. There are several practices for the view-through conversion window such as 3-days, although the 24 hour window is probably the best.

The 24-hour window gives you data about the quality of your ad placements, stickiness of your ads, users shopping habits, and to doesn't overstate or inflate the effectiveness of the advertisement.

6.) Ensure you have a Single Retargeting Provider

There are many companies out there offering retargeting services. There are drawbacks to using more than one provider for you retargeting campaigns.

Each provider bids for the same spots where the ads will be on the website which increases the costs of those ads. It also decreases the chances that each provider has to serve your ads to your users. You will have difficulties with the implementation of frequency caps if you do this as each retargeting provider is independent.

It's better to use just one targeting provider, even if you're new to this as you'll get better results over the course of several months. You'll be able to see if the campaign worked without having skewed results because you used too many providers.

7.) Make Sure You Optimize Your Images and Creatives

One factor that will determine your success overall all others is the actual banner ads that you use. You want to ensure you have great looking advertisements. You don't want to jam the banner ad full of information as this ends up distracting your audience which isn't your intention and ruins the purpose of the ad.

The goal is to get their attention and to keep their attention. The experience should be a rewarding one for the user and even if they don't click on the ad, the brand awareness stays with them long after they have viewed the ad.

A simple ad and minimal copy is the best way to go. You want the ad to be recognizable and well-branded. You want concise copy, bold colors, and a clear call to action as well as clickable buttons.

You don't want to run the same ad for months on end as this results in a lower performing campaign. A retargeter study showed the there's a 50% decrease after five months if the same ads are run. If the user sees the same ads there's no interest there anymore and the ads tend to blend into the background for the user.

8.)Use A/B Tests to Increase Performance

You want to rotate the ads every few months as this will help you avoid the dips in ad performance. You can use what we call A/B tests that can give you data to run your campaigns with ads that work. A/B tests is nothing more than running same ads with very slight differences in 2 groups just so you keep checking which one works better and get better conversion, so as you keep doing the A/B tests, you keep improving your results since you are constantly testing what the consumers are responding to .

You'll have actionable and measureable results that give you results. If you use A/B testing on your creatives you will figure out the best combination for your ad copy, graphics, and call-to-action. Retargeter always runs A/B tests and we recommend that you do the same to ensure the best results for your ads.

Retargeting your Website

Your website is critical to your online presence. You use it to direct traffic, communicate your value to users, it proves the feel and look of your brand, and it's where you optimize for SEO. All marketing leads back to your website. Once you get that traffic you have to be concerned about what happens once that traffic leaves your site.

When you use website retargeting you don't have to be as concerned about that traffic after it leaves our website. Site retargeting will display ads to this people that have left your site and are visiting other websites.

This method ensures that you don't lose all that traffic and reminds visitors to come back and visit your site again to do more research or to make a purchase.

Retargeting Your Email
One of your most important marketing channels is email. In a survey over 77% of uses prefer email messages to other forms of communication. You already do email marketing so email retargeting is a supplement to this. You can increase the reach of email campaigns with this method.

You'll be able to reduce shopping cart abandonment, upsell to your existing customers drive offline actions, and promote limited time offers when you use email retargeting. When you don't use email retargeting, you're leaving it up to the mailing list subscribers to take the next steps. Internet users do prefer email message, but you'll get more results with display in combination with email. This can lead to more website traffic and traffic to your landing page.

Measuring the Success of Your Retargeting

Your goals are going to determine the success you have with retargeting emails. Your outcome may differ from that of another marketer. Before you start your campaign, you need to determine what you want out of the campaign and then set your metrics for this.

Digital advertising has an advantage over more traditional media as it can directly attribute sales to ad impressions. Some think that clicks are one of the common indictors of success, but this is an action that can be measured, but clicks are not as accurate when it comes to display. Advertisements don't usually create an immediate purchasing decision.

Most advertisements are produced to influence consumer behavior so they buy at some point in the future and not the present. It's hard to judge whether seeing an advertisement will make someone buy in the future.

Many Internet users don't click on advertisements at all and it doesn't matter the demographic of the con-clickers vs. the clickers as there's a significant percentage of people that just don't click at all, but they are still influenced by advertising. A recent study said that seeing an advertisement does help with conversion and it can convert a person who might not otherwise click on ads unclicked ads are still very valuable to your campaign so it's wise to invest in ads even though they don't get clicked.

These channels can still drive a lot of revenue although they might not seem to because of unclicked advertisements.

Choosing a Retargeting Provider

You need time, know-how and knowledge to launch a successful retargeting campaign. A self-serve retargeting provider allows you to manage the campaign on your own. You'll create the banner ads, optimize across networks, and choose how much you'll spend. If you have the resources and the time, this sort of retargeting campaign is for you.

If you go with a full service provider then your account is managed for you. An experienced manager will look after the campaign and you'll get a good return on your investment this way. It's going to cost you more, but this is usually worth your investment to do so. It's up to you to decide which method is going to work the best for your campaign.

Oguz Konar

61

CHAPTER 3

Online Reputation

Ratings and reviews on 3rd party sites are important to your success. If you have more ratings you tend to be ranked higher on the search engines. People that are potential buyers are trusting reviews and ratings from a 3rd party website as they are doing more research prior to making purchases or buying services.

They look to reviews on sites like Yelp, Angie's List, Google+, Trip Advisor, Avvo, UrbanSpoon and similar sites.

You need a string offense to combat narrative reviews. You want to ensure that you have more positive than negative reviews.

If you don't currently have any reviews then you're gambling a bit and you could quickly get a negative reputation without any positive reviews to lessen the impact of that negative review on your site.

Reviews are increasingly more influential in getting new customer to try new products, purchase services, and shop at local businesses. Here are some of our clients and evidence of this for you to review:

- A local chiropractor asks new patients if they have ever heard of his practice. Over the last year he says that the number of patients that said they got a referral from a review site went from 40 to 80 percent.
- A spa had a lot of great reviews and was getting plenty of new clients. They launched a Groupon daily deal to grow their business. The deal brought in many new clients, but the staff wasn't ready for this new influx. They ended up providing poor service and as a result, had a lot of new poor reviews listed. The owner needed to stop the business to deal with the crisis and to repair their on line reputation.

- Two pizza joints are competing with each other in a town with a large restaurant turnover and a dining scent that is picky. One of the owners decides to use a "black hat" technique and get a lot of fake reviews. Our clients decides to get actual honest reviews from customers each month. Our client has seen a steady growing business with busy nights and packed weekend patrons. The competitor has empty five star reviews and only two reviews from actual customers saying the 5 star reviews are phony.

This shows how much impact "social proof" can have for your business in today's marketplace. Consumers validate how well your business is by making reviews online which can positively or negatively impact how well your business does. It's not easy to build your social proof, but these results are well worth the investment. It's the "age of the consumer," according to Forrester Research. Consumers today are very demanding and you need to ensure that you provide the best service for them possible to **ensure your online reputation stays positive. Consumers today are 72% more likely to trust reviews online left by**

strangers as much as they will when recommendations come from friends or family.

1. It doesn't matter if you're taking about a contractor, medical practice, restaurant or any other type of business, customer reviews are very important. It's perceived that the reviews are left by regular people that have no agenda and people have come to trust these reviews and even more so than expert opinions. In 2011, a study found that consumers felt that the opinions of "others like me," were valuable 55% of the time and impacts on their decisions to buy.

2. This point can be seen in the popular website Ange's list. In 2011 they began to use the tagline "Reviews you can trust, written by people just like you." Since this time the trust of reviews have risen globally. In the 2012 Nielsen survey called "Global Trust in Advertising Survey," online reviews trusted reviews of people they didn't know 70% of the time which is up from four years prior. It's said that 92% of consumers from around the world trust

word-of-mouth recommendations and it doesn't matter if this is friends, family, or even strangers. This is above all other types of advertising methods.

3. People that tend to leave reviews are wealthier, younger, and have an optimistic view on technology which is the new marketing segment.

P.S. We have a BONUS video about our 5 Star Reputation Management System. If you'd like know how we automate this process for your clients, so you can keep collecting positive reviews and get it posted on the sites that matter (Google+, Yelp, etc.),

If you are interested, you can watch the video at www.localmarketingstars.com

Oguz Konar

67

CHAPTER 4

Understanding Social Media: The Breakdown

What exactly is Social Media?

Social media is based upon mobile and web based technology and turns our communication into a dialogue that is interactive. Some examples of social media include Twitter, Facebook, Google+, LinkedIn, and YouTube. Social media is then basically using social networks to communicate, build relationships, and engage with others.

Although you don't necessarily need a presence on all of the social networks, (we highly recommend you do) but you can't ignore the presence of social media and it can help your business develop.

Why Should I use Social Media?

You may think that social media isn't as important for your type of business, but this isn't the case at all. About 65% of all U.S. adults

have at least one social media account.
Facebook just isn't for fans of the latest rock
band.

Facebook for example, has its own
search engine and hundreds of millions of
people use it every month and every day. You
need to get in front of your target market and if
they are on these sites, then you need to be as
well.

All sorts of individuals use these social
media sites such as students, prospective
clients, and your colleagues. In a survey it said
that 77% of college students had one social
media account or more. You can benefit from
social media in regard to media placement,
getting new clients, and recruiting. One New
Jersey Real Estate Law Firm has a Facebook
page it uses to recruit new law firm students. It
posts funny video that showcases the friendly
atmosphere, legal alerts, as well as new job
postings. It can connect with new students in
the way that regular campus recruiting simply
can't.

Another Dentist in New York that
specializes in cosmetic dentistry uses Twitter to
post new patients and show before and after
images to attract new patients to its business.

There's a lot of value for your business to use social media whether you're a one man show or a larger business.

What Is Social Media For?

You really can't consider social media just for personal use. It's more than silly updates about your dog or your latest trip news. It's important for businesses to use social media more for business than just personal use. If you do use it for personal reasons then have a separate account for that purpose. Professional accounts should be kept professional as your reputation is on the line. You can use social media for a bit of your personal life but keep it at about 70/30. The personal posts should be of the tame variety.

You want to have respect and a solid reputation and clients, customers and patients will look at your social media profiles to find out more about you. If you feel theirs is need to share personal things in your social media account, open a new one for your personal life. It really all depends on your goal and who you want to attract. How you manage your account is up to you, but professional is always best.

Social Networks

Social networks are all different and it doesn't have to be intimidating to set up even if you haven't use them before. The people you associate in social networks will probably all be different from each other and you'll discuss different topics and post different things on each one of the sites.

Don't overwhelm yourself with too much on the various sites. Or the other option would be to outsource your social media management to professionals.

Facebook

Facebook can be considered the giant of the social networks and it's estimated that over 1 billion minutes per month are spent by Americans on the social network. People talk about adventures, post latest photographs, look at what employees are saying about work, and so on. Each day about 800 million worldwide are logged into Facebook.

Facebook has increased its search abilities to take advantage of this and is actually competing with Google in this regard. Facebook doesn't want you to leave the site because of its advertisers which makes it easier for people to stay on the site. Go to Facebook now and type in the search bar which is at the top of the page and type the name of your law firm.

On the results page you'll get results from inside of Facebook And outside of Facebook too. If your business had its own Facebook page, this would be listed at the top of the results for clients, patients and customers to find and access. This works just as well for keyword searches like "injury lawyer", "emergency dentist in Morristown New Jersey" or "plumber in x city" as examples.

You need to be selective about what you do or do not post on Facebook. Try to make the post appropriate like your company's news, pictures of you at your company event, you supporting a charity, and so on. Keep the posts business specific and you'll do fine.

LinkedIn

For business professionals, LinkedIn is the way to go. This site is like a one-page resume for you and your business. You can share you latest achievements or an article you published, for example. The site makes it easy to connect with other like-minded professionals so you can expand upon your recognition. The site says there are over 300 million users on the site engaging with other professionals, sharing insights, accessing knowledge, as well as opportunities.

When you share the posts with care and use social media etiquette, this site can be a great asset to your business to remind others that you have a thriving and great business worth investigating or referring to others. Make sure what you share is geared towards other professionals.

Think in terms of: would another colleague want to see or read this material? A recent court victory for example, would be of interest to potential clients who is interested in same services and products.

This is the type of impression that you want to establish on the site. Google ranks LinkedIn quite high in search results and often it's on the first page of results. This means that when a client, media member or someone else type your name into Google, the LinkedIn profile will most likely be at the top of the search results page. When someone does click this link you want them to be impressed by your LinkedIn profile so you want to have a professional photograph and a full profile available to them.

Don't post cute photographs as this isn't professional and not the right choice for this site, so make sure you have a full and up-to-date professional profile on the site. A good profile will go a long way to establishing your reputation on the site and with new clients.

Twitter

Family, coworkers, and friends use Twitter. This site is for frequent and short messages. On this site as a small business you can expand your global reach to new potential clients without paying for the huge costs of an advertisement campaign. Sponsored Tweets can be an option which show up in a competitor's newsfeed, but you don't have to go this route.

The media uses Twitter as a portal to share news, and provide the latest breaking stories, for example. For a local business, there's great potential as the site has over 600 million active users and I am sure millions in your local area. You have direct access to the media as well as clients and partners, all with 140 characters or less.

You can use the site to engage, share links, and to communicate as much as you like. The best part of Twitter is the ability to "retweet" what others have to say which increases the sharing on posts. People use retweets to create a buzz about something.

During the Oscar's Ellen DeGeneres had a goal to shut down Twitter with the retweet of her "celebrity selfie," and this actually worked. Your tweets probably won't case this sort of buzz, but it shows just how powerful retweet can be to reach new people who in turn may show an interest in you.

The goal is to create a buzz with your retweets to get more people to see what you have to say. You do want to consider etiquette here and the goal is to "uplift" others. So by replying to tweets, favoring them and retweeting posts you like from your colleagues, you in turn help yourself.

This increases the exposure of not only the other party, but of you as well across Twitter. There's a boost in search engine optimization or SEO that both of you want

Google + Local

Mobile searches usually come from Google. To fond local businesses Google created Google+ Local. This makes it easy for local business to connect with people interested in what they have to offer.

Google+ Local works well on mobile pages and is integrated with Google Maps one of the most popular apps. You can even integrate Google+ Local with Google AdWords which enhances a PPC campaign.

It's free to setup Google+ Local pages, but you need to ensure they are connected with your website to get good results. You want to verify your page, connect the website, and have pick the right categories.

You also want to have a good keyword description of your business and related services you offer. For your listing you want reviews and images as these are an important part of the listing. You want to take time with this and encourage new users to leave reviews whenever possible.

You don't want to ignore this social media site as it has the power of Google behind it. It's not as popular as Twitter or Facebook, but it has perks which the other two sites do not. You have the ability to use Google authorship. When you do a search you may find articles which have an image of the author attached to that article in a little avatar.

This allows the write of that article to attach their blog or website to their Google+ account. This increases search engine optimization and it also establishes trust and familiarity with the reader. The person that is using Google to look for information can connect the information they are reading with the author. The benefits offered by Google Authorship are well worth the signup.

If you use Google+ for a social aspect the results do end up in the Google search results so Google+ is a great way to highlight blog posts, legal achievements, and other endeavors that are professional in nature which helps your business. Some may find that Google+ isn't as user-friendly as Facebook or Twitter as a way to connect but Google does offer an easy way to do this and it's called Google Hangouts.

These are chat facilities and it's easy to use it to connect to your various offices, for example on different coasts and you don't need complicated video conferring services to do this.

CHAPTER 5

PPC Campaigns through GOOGLE and SEO

Google Lead Generation to Leverage AdWords Power to Grow Your Small Business Quickly

If you're looking for success in your local business, then Google AdWords is here to help you do just that. AdWords is a great opportunity to increase your profits and grow your business. This is a unique advertising platform unlike any you have previously used before. If you want to generate leads for your business and grow your bottom line, then this guide is going to help you out.

Local businesses with a physical location that want to dominate online with their services are going to have a huge advantage with Google AdWords. There's a real opportunity with this advertising platform that you're going to learn about.

When you're trying to grow your business, everything you do with marketing has to have real and measurable results. This is different than a big ad agency creating campaigns for a fast food chain, for example. The marketplace and your niche come into play, but these strategies and tips are going to help you see real growth with your law firm and practice

Google AdWords Foundation

Traditionally, billboards, newspaper ads, radio spots, and television commercials, have bene the route to gain leads and exposure for small business. These types of advertising are what we call "Interruption Advertising." The goal is to interrupt as many people as possible to get your message across and hopefully a few of them will be interested in what you have to say.

These methods are old and they just aren't as effective as Google AdWords is at getting your message across to those that matter to you.

If someone in your local area does a Google search for your type of business then that is a good lead that you want to have. If they find your ad at the top of the page, click on it and call you, you have a potential new client. Many people are using Google to find a business because of the need for those services. The searcher is not thinking of the future here, they are thinking of the right now usually. That person is in the middle of the buying process so this sort of advertisement works better than the "Interruption Advertising," which is annoying to most people because they don't need your services right now and aren't thinking of one.

You want someone that is in the prices of wanting something, not thinking of this in the future. Having someone find you when they need you is a lot better than doing a "cold call "or "interrupting" busy people with your advertisement. For this reason Google AdWords is very powerful.

The lead you get from Google AdWords is 100% measurable so you know what you'll be getting on your investment. You don't know what you'll be getting when you use more traditional forms of advertising. Google AdWords allows you to reach people that are already looking for a business like your and are wanting to buy from that business and in this case, the services of a lawyer like yourself.

The ads you deliver to people are morel likely going to turn up a lead than other forms of advertising and it's therefore not wasted money. Google AdWords is the best thing to happen to the world of Advertising and for small businesses specifically, it can be an absolute goldmine.

It's possible to build a multimillion dollar businesses if you're an entrepreneurial business owner by using Google AdWords and many have done just that. It's the primary way many small businesses generate new business. And you'll see that it can do amazing things for your own business as well.

Using Google AdWords to Generate Online Leads

Google makes its money through AdWords which is its advertising platform and not thoorugh regular search results. Google wants you to advertise with them and they want you to get the results you're looking for. The whole idea is to get you to spend money with them year after year.

Most small businesses have the wrong idea that people don't click on Google AdWords at the top of the search results, but this isn't the case at all. Many people click on the second or the third seeded result all the time. Many people don't even know that the first few results are in fact, actual ads and not plain searches.

You only need a small percentage of people to click on your ads to generate more leads for your business than you ever thought possible before. If you're not willing to make an investment into an AdWords campaign you are throwing away a lot of potential clients and solid lead generation.

SEO, or search engine optimization is a strategy that's longer-term as it takes a lot of effort as well as money to rank high in the search engines for valuable keywords. If you're a new business or a start-up, you will not rank high in search engines immediately, it will take time, time that you might not have to wait for SEO to catch up to you, (although you need SEO as well)

You won't rank high because every other lawyer that is just out of law school in your local area is trying to do the same thing you are. In addition to this, all the other established businesses already have a good online presence so you're SEO is probably not going to make much difference as there's already a ton of competition. Many established small businesses have been using SEO for years and have their high rankings which you're not going to our rank in any short period of time.

Many of these attorneys spend thousands of dollars each year for their SEO campaigns and still don't rank well in the engines because there's just so many attorneys out there doing the same thing. The main problem is that you actually need a page one rank for anyone to even recognize you and if you aren't, then you won't get a whole lot of organic leads your way.

On the other hand, if you invest in Google AdWords, you can get great results. You could potentially get new clients, customers and patients and leads right away instead of waiting for search traffic and placement that may or may not come.

You could wait weeks or even years just to even get a decent placement on Google and in many cases, it simply never happens. By Using Google AdWords you can get clients and then reinvest that money into buying additional advertising for your growing business.

Google also changes its search algorithm quit often so all that money you spend in SEO is worthless after a few months and you have to change everything all over again. When you invest in Google AdWords, you're getting traffic that's' already interested in what you have to offer.

You can get to the top of the rankings with tons of different keywords and variations when you use Google AdWords and not just a few like you do with regular SEO. You get the leads you want right away with AdWords and it pays for itself. Television, radio, newspapers, and billboards simply don't provide you the tangible results that Google AdWords does.

All those older forms of advertising are also very expensive and there's no guarantee it will even pay off for you in the long run. You could waste thousands of dollars on hardly any results. You would be better off investing that money into AdWords.

When you use AdWords you can run a test campaign for a week to see how it performs for you. It might just take a few hundred dollars to see some good results from your campaign. A t the end of the week, you'll get a lot of data that tells you how well the campaign worked, how many leads you received, the number of clicks, and the new clients you received along with other valuable information you can use to make the next campaign even better.

You can then split-test as and decide how you want to proceed with your campaign in terms of funds you want to spend. If you spend say $1,000 and make back $5,000, then you're doing well. The nest month you can spend that $5,000 on advertising and you can make even more profit this way.

If you're looking for measurable results that are reliable all the time then you want to be using AdWords. The next section will discuss how you can use AdWords to create a great AdWords campaign that's effective for you. If you run one now this section will help you make the campaign even better than it is already for you.

Dominate Local Advertising with Google AdWords

Local businesses can make Google AdWords work for them. Google loves to showcase a local business and you can integrate Google+ Local with your AdWords account. When people search for your business in the local area your ad is displayed in a larger size and the phone number as address are displayed right there for the potential client to view.

If the ad is larger, people are going to notice this. They are going to want to read the details of the ad and they're going to actually click on the ad and visit you. If you integrate the Google+ Local account, then the location information is displayed along with the ad. You're going to end up with more leads and desire for your services. If you take the time to integrate your Google+ Local account, then this is going to improve the bottom line of your business.

Another factor that will help your campaign is to split-test ads to find ones that get the best CTR or click through rate. Many small businesses that try Google AdWords fail because they don't have a good landing page and they haven't tested multiple ads to get a better click through rate. If you have a good AdWords campaign and are generating plenty of clicks going to your business, Google will reward you with a cheaper cost-per-click. This means Google thinks you're relevant and it's a reward for having a good AdWords ad and campaign that's successful.

If you continue to get a solid CTR, then the rate for the clicks will keep going down. It's easier for people to click on your ad with Google and you're generating more business as well as saving money on your clicks with Google AdWords.

The nest part will deal with common mistakes that people make. You'll learn how to have a successful AdWords campaign so you get leads.

Use these Strategies to Improve Your AdWords Conversions

If you're ready to give AdWords a try, this section is for you. If you are ready to pay attention to your campaign and really work on it then you're going to do well with Google AdWords. Here are bad habits that you need to avoid.

You are probably think about where the clicks are going to go and what website or pages to use. You might think that your expensive website is going to draw in the clients and users to your business, but this isn't the case. You can actually lose clients if you send them to your full website.

What you need to do is to send the traffic to your landing page. This is a simple and easy to read single page that invites your potential new clients and prospects to take immediate action.

A landing page is designed to draw the interest of the client before they get too distracted and leave the page. If you simply send the traffic to the main website then it's far easier for the potential new client to get distracted because of information overload.

Your website probably has tons of sections and the client can easily lose track of where they are and simply leave the site. The client doesn't fill out a contact form or doesn't call you so you lose out on that lead.

You want to have high-converting landing pages with a good template because you want your prospects to pick up the phone and give you a call.

Here are three marketing mistakes that you want to avoid:

- Make sure you split-test advertisements. You might be getting clicks and some business, but you could be doing better so check the performance of the ads.
- Have a high-converting landing page. Your main website may look great, but it won't draw in prospective clients as there's too much for them to do on the site. A landing page grabs the attention of the reader right away so they pick up the phone and schedule an appointment with you.
- Make sure you setup your AdWords campaign correctly. A proper setup of the campaign is going to be critical to your success with the program.

I love the Google AdWords platform for the simple reasons that it offers you so much potential. Google is the largest search engine in the world and it offers users access to just so much information, but it's also the number one way to market yourself as an attorney.

Google has grown over the past few years and it's not going to go anywhere. AdWords is only goin got improve which is going to mean more money and new clients for you. If you're not using Google right now, then you're being left behind so get on AdWords as soon as you can.

SEO Services

You need to have SEO or basic search engine optimization. Goof SEO will help you position your website on Google so people will find it during the critical parts of the buying process they are in.

So what exactly are the search engines looking for?

How can you establish your site on Goggle, Bing, Yahoo, and other search engines to maximize your exposure online?

How can SEO increase your profits?

The SEO session was intended for new people to the business, but her tips were very important for even professionals who have been working with SEO for years and already optimizing websites.

So What is SEO?

You don't want to game the search engines by using SEO as this won't work. The main purpose of SEO is to:

- Create a seamless user experience.
- Tell the search engines your intentions so the engines can recommend your website for the relevant searches or your keywords.

What the Search Engines Look For

A search engine is looking for the most relevant content on a subject that the user of the search engine is looking for. How is this relevancy determined by the search engine?

- **Content.** The theme of the website, the descriptions, titles, and txt on the page are important to the search engine.
- **Performance.** The site needs to work properly and be fast.
- **Authority.** The site needs to have great content and to link to other content which is an authority on the subject. There needs to be references or citation of the content presented.
- **User experience.** The site has to be well presented and easy to navigate. The site should be safe for users and it shouldn't have a high bounce rate.

What Search Engines Don't Look For...
Search engine spiders store a certain amount of data. If you try to trick them or use shady practices to try and game the s each engines, you're just going to hurt yourself over time. Search engines don't want the following:

- **Keyword stuffing.** This is overusing keywords on the page.

- **Purchased links.** If you buy links in an attempt to get a better rank with SEO, this will backfire on you.
- **Poor user experience.** You have to make it easy for the user to move around your website. If there's too many advertisements this will cause people to leave the website and you'll have a bad bounce rate. If your bounce rate is 80% or higher you're doing something wrong with your site.

Understand Your Business Model
This might seem obvious, but many people don't write down their goals. Some questions you need to ask include:

- How do you define a conversion for your business?
- Are you selling clicks or impressions?
- DO you have an understanding of your liabilities as well as your assets?
- Do you know your goals?

Make Sure You Optimize for Many Channels

You need keyword strategy for your site, but this should also carry over to other off-site platforms. You need to optimize over many channels which may include:

- Twitter
- Email
- Facebook
- Offline, like radio or television

When using these platforms, you need to ensure that your keywords are kept consistent. This will help your branding efforts and users will be trained to use the phrases that you want to have optimized.

Domain Names need to be Consistent

Domain names are very important so you need to be suing sub-directory root names like: (yoursite.com/greatcontent) and not sub-

domains which would be
(greatcontet.yoursite.com.)

- If you type in www.yoursite.com, but
  then just yoursiite.com and the www
  part doesn't direct you to
  www.yoursite.com., the search engines
  are seeing two different sites. This isn't
  been beneficial to your SEO efforts and
  causes your inbound links to be diluted.
  The sites will be linking to both
  www.yoursite.com and yoursiite.com.
- Keep the domain old school. You want
  to use older domain names if possible. If
  you buy these older domains make sure
  the domain doesn't have any problems
  with it such as shady practices by the
  previous owner as the domain may
  already have a penalty attached to it.
- URL Keywords. Try to have keywords in
  the URL as this will help your overall
  ranking efforts with that website.

Optimizing for Different Types of Results

You need to ensure that the site is
optimized for different devices like tablets as
well as smartphones and other media too.

- You need great media content like videos. It's easier to get a video to rank on the first page of Google than an article with the same content.
- You want the non-text content to be optimized so search engines are able to see this. If the site uses PDFs or Flash, make sure you use the best practices so the search engines can crawl this content so your site gets credit for it.

The Meta Data Needs Focus as Well

Make sure your website has both title tag and Meta descriptions.

- Meta keywords are usually ignored by search engines now, but if you're using them make sure they focus on the page and that everything is formatted properly.
- The Meta description need to be unique and it should also speak of the specific page. You don't want duplicate Meta data on pages as this leads to nowhere for your website.

You need to have a unique title tag. This is like a 4-8 word advertisement for your website. You want to entice the reader to come into the site to take a look around.

You need to keep SEO in mind and follow the best practices for using it. You can't skip the basics of SEO and expect your website to do well online.

If you skip good SEO, your revenue will decline and the foundation of your site will be a mess which just drops your search engine ranking making it difficult to get it back again.

P.S. More than 85% of our clients who are using our other solutions are using our SEO service to have their websites perform at the highest levels and diminish the competition. Contact us for our packages if interested.

The Ultimate Guide to Online Marketing

CHAPTER 6

Video Marketing

Videos are more popular than ever and in the future, you're going to see more of them online than ever. It's said that by 2017, videos will make up about 69% of all the consumer traffic online according to Cisco. All statistics on the subject of video show that it's just growing rapidly and this is going to continue which means you simply can't afford to leave video out of your marketing plans.

If you leave out video, you're not going to see the growth that you could see if you had included video in your marketing plans. This is especially true for small businesses which face a lot of competition online.

Videos will be the future of content marketing. It's said that over half of companies are already using videos in some form or another for their own businesses and the figure just keeps going up.

According to Nielsen, marketers expect video to be a big part of their marketing strategies in the near future and it's clear to see why this is the case.

When it comes to reach, there's nothing that beats a good video. Over one billion unique users visit YouTube each month and this more than any other channel except Facebook. In United States, 1 in 3 visit the site at least once per week, so there's a weekly audience of 20 million just in the U.S. Video can help you reach all these users and no other content form is able to do what video is able to do for your growing business.

Many video campaigns are the thing of legend as they go viral online. One recent campaign from Volkswagen as an example, saw three of its videos viewed 155 million times. These numbers may out of reach for smaller companies, but they show the potential of videos, because they get shared amongst users and with those users' friends. A person viewing a video will spend more time on your website and will interact with your brand for a longer time. For any social media campaign or SEO exercise, video is one of the bets things you can possibly use for more exposure.

Consumers face information overload online and videos give them small segments that they can quickly digest. If consumers don't get easily to digest content, they will move on quickly.

Videos help to fill this role of quick, informative content for the viewer. According to Axonn Research, 7 in 10 people had a more positive view of a brand after they viewed video content provided by that brand.

Using video s possible for a small business and it should be used. The costs of making videos has dropped significantly in recent years and you don't need to be a technical expert to make a great looking video.

There's great apps such as Twitter's Vine which allows for a quick six-second clip have opened up opportunities for companies with a limited budget to get started. To maximize the return on your investment, you need to consider the following.

The video should always be relevant to the audience you're trying to reach. If the vide isn't the right way to get the message to them, then it's not a good idea to use the video in the first place.

Social media has a lot of potential so ensure that your clips are shown there. It should be easy for users to find the video and then to share it. You should also ensure you're suing mobile too. According to Ooyala, a tenth of all videos are played on mobile devices like tablets and smartphones.

This is a segment that's growing and in June 2013, there was a 41% more video consumption when compare dot the start of the year which shows that video use is continuing upward at a rapid pace.

Your videos should also be creative, in both the campaign and the video that you make. Being creative is a lot better than simply having a slick expensive production. If you get video right, it will be the future of all your content marketing so work on it and produce the best videos possible as they are important to the future growth of your business.

Explainer Videos

One way to jumpstart your conversion rates is to use explainer videos. These videos are fun to make and are perfect for any startup business.

An explainer video is a short video that explain the service or product of your company. These are often placed on a landing page, a prominent product page, or the home page of your website.

These are very popular and it can increase conversion rates by as much as 144% once you have once established one on your website. These videos are a great asset to your business and it's easy to get your own explainer video.

Types of Videos Ideal for Small Businesses;

- **In Person Videos.** These videos are non-animated and explain a business's service or product. These live action videos are best suited for companies that have a physical product or a service that's people oriented like a consulting group or a restaurant.

     You want to have real people in your explainer video as this can create a connection with your viewers. Make sure you keep the video in the real world so no magical or fantasy type videos as this will just confuse the viewer.

- **Animated Videos.** These are a very popular type of explainer video. For explaining services, or tech products such as software, animation videos work great. If a service doesn't involve many physical objects then animation videos may not work that well.

When you use animation videos they allow for more creativity and they are easy to update or edit making future adjustments to the video a breeze.

- **Whiteboard animation videos.** This type of video is where an animation is drawn by hand and then erased on a whiteboard. This video is lower cost and easy to use and is the cheapest type of explainer video that you can create which is perfect for small businesses just trying to get a head start.

- **Kickstarter Explainer Videos.** All Kickstarter projects involve an explainer video of some type or another. These videos aren't that different from regular service or product videos, but tend to be longer.

By going to Kickstarter and browsing their site, you can see many examples there of explainer style videos.

> If you need videos for your business to grow your following, sell more products or build your authority in your market, contact us to find out more about our video marketing packages. info@localmarketingstars.com

Chapter 7

Direct Mail Marketing

THE CENTURY OLD IDEA

The concept of direct mailing is far from being a new concept. It has been around for many many years and has been perfected by the masters of sales copy and marketing as time goes. The method we based the foundations of our direct mailing system comes from the Real Estate industry originally.

They use a method called "farming" to generate the lead that over time turn into sales for the real estate agent. In basic terms the real estate agent exerts and intense and a concentrated effort to become the dominant individual in his/her expertise in a small and a carefully selected market.

A "farm" is a geographic, demographic or psychographic defined list of prospects. As a small business you have a number of farms available to you and I would like you to consider working each of these farms.

1. **The existent customer base for referrals.** This is considered a "warm list" and the conversion rate of this list is a lot higher than mailing letters to a "cold list".

2. **A selective geographic area**, a neighborhood or a subdivision near your business. According to statistics, more the 97% of your customers will be generated from 3 miles radius of your physical locations (if you have a physical location).

3. **New residents to a given area.** In order to search for that, you can go possibly scan a larger area around your business than defined in the selected geographic area or the neighborhood farm.

4. **Networking groups** such as your Chamber of Commerce, BNI Groups, La Tip, the church or another religious organization you belong to, other clubs and associations that you are a part of. Belonging to one of these groups is the first step of a successful lead generation system.

A Little Tip On Networking

a.) A little Networking Tip: Taking action and joining the meetings shows your commitment and your dedication to growing your practice.

b.) The second step would be to say the right things that would grab the attention of people interacting with you. Invariable people will ask what you do for a living, and answering that question with a mere "Well, I am a chiropractor/dentist/plumber etc" would be the most banal thing you can do. That statement doesn't separate you from the other similar businesses in the room, does it?

If I were to need a chiropractor and asked you that question and you gave me the good old "I am a chiropractor" answer, What exactly would be my reason to choose you as my chiropractor over other people in the room?

SEQUENCE YOUR WAY TO WEALTH

SEQUENCING METHOD

We always begin by planting the farm with a sequence of letters, each referring to the previous letter. And this is a critically important concept. Most people who complain about getting poor results from direct mail start shooting themselves in the foot right from the very beginning by mailing only one time to a given group of prefects and once just isn't enough. One shot direct mail rarely works.

Why? Well there are many reasons. For one thing, we're all very busy and preoccupied people. We sort our mail on the run, over the waste basket, and we're bombarded by advertising stuff every waking minute at the office and at home. But big time advertisers know that it takes massive repetition to even get our attention. You can't match them dollar for dollar but you can take the core of their approach, the repetition part, and use it wisely and strategically.

By mailing to the same prospects repeatedly in a strategically timed and themed sequence rather that once or once in a blue moon, you immediately and clearly stand out as different from all other advertisers and all other marketers, you become a known entity quickly. You even become a topic of conversation.

When you plant the farm with a sequence of 3 letters, we call this the 3-step letter system, each referring to the previous letters, we are essentially saying, "Hey there! We are here for you, here's who we are, and you're going to be hearing from us a lot. We're here to stay to serve you and we're not going anywhere." You're making a positioning statement, staking a claim on a territory, making an impact.

<u>The sequence works like this:</u>

1.) Letter #1 goes out to everybody in a selective farm area,

2.) Then 15 days later, everybody who has not responded gets Letter #2.

3.) Then 15 days later, everybody in the farm area who has not responded gets Letter #3,

4.) Then 15 days later they get Letter #4.

In 60 days, these people have heard from you four times. The second and third contacts have referred to the previous contacts. By the time they get the third letter, people will be talking about you.

The wives will be showing the letters to the husbands, the husbands will be showing the letters to the wives, neighbors will be asking each other about the letters. If you live or stay in the farm area, you will be recognized. You will have had a major impact on the residents of this farm area. I sometimes compare this sequence to a collection letter sequence, a <u>collection letter sequence</u>. If you've ever been behind in paying your bills at sometime in your life, you've gotten collection letters, and usually each letter refers to the previous letter in the sequence, and each letter gets a little tougher than the previous one.

The sequence usually peaks with a final notice. Just about every collection effort, every company, every collection company, every collection attorney uses this strategy. Why do they do that? Because it works! Of course, we are not contacting them about the bills they are behind, but we are using the same philosophy with a positive spin to it where they can hugely benefit from your services.

Now if you'll examine the plant-the-farm letters, you'll see that they offer a free gift.

This tool is very important. When you communicate with, say one hundred people, only a few may have back pain or a headache or a toothache that particular day. Few may have a clearly perceived need for your services at the minute of your communication so most of your communication effort is wasted. It never has a chance. Therefore we need to do something about it. We have to eliminate this waste;

To do that, we have to change the offer we are communicating so that it is relevant and of interest to just about everybody at the moment it gets delivered, whether they have a perceived need for your services at that moment or not. <u>We have to change the purpose of our communication from getting a new patient to starting a new relationship.</u>

This process is designed to start relationships not just to immediately get new patients. You almost certainly will get many many new patients, but that's not the main purpose or the payoff. The main purpose or the payoff is starting relationships so we can sustain relationships so that when the time comes when that person does have a need for services or they know someone who does, your name will already be engraved in their brain, when the need arises and becomes clearly perceived, they already have a relationship with you, and naturally, automatically comes to you.

By offering a desirable free gift, we encourage everybody to respond now, regardless of whether or not they have a perceived immediate need for our services. By responding and getting our free gift, they initiate a relationship. The more relationships we start, the more customers you'll get.

STATISTICS NEVER LIE

How effective is direct mail marketing?

Well.. there are so many possible answers to this question to prove the unmatched effectiveness of direct mailing.

However nothing is better than working with actual statistics to make our point, instead of spending hours explaining whether it will work for you or not.

Let's not waste time but dive right into some of the statistics based on a recent research;

- 62% of people like to receive mail telling them about new offers.

- More than 50% of the mail goes to garbage without being opened. Obviously, if your mail looks like JUNK, acts like JUNK, smells like

JUNK, 50% of them will be treated like junk. Module 2 reveals how NOT to be a Junk Mailer.

- 70% of people welcome mail that rewards their loyalty.

That's why many department stores keep sending you coupons through mail. Touching and feeling to a "10% OFF coupon" is proven to leave a deeper psychological footprint in our brain that receiving the same material through e mail . There article on this study is also attached under your bonus content.

56% of people welcome mail that gives them useful information.

The ARR (Average Response Rate) for direct mailing ranges from 3.4% to 4.4%.

- 88% of the respondents to a recent survey state that they will use direct mailing for their business in the next 12 months.

Since many people are going delirious about using social media for their business to reach their clients as a means of their total marketing strategy, the direct mail marketing has been going through its least competitive time period. With the sales letters provided to you in this system, you will take advantage of this low competitive environment to maximize the number of patients.

- 25% of the direct mailing pieces that are opened by the recipient are kept at his/her house for 30 days on average. (Talk about being in front of your potential client all the time.)

Marketing with a Tearsheet mailing will generally double your stay-home rate.

What is a tearsheet?

It's a great marketing letter that presents a story printed on a newspaper style print making it look like it was actually ripped from a newspaper with a personal note on it. People love to keep that kind of unique information

Direct Mailing Statistic Based On The Age Ranges

15 – 19

- 32% of them responded to Direct Mail.

- 79% will open direct mail that is deemed to contain relevant information.

16 – 24

- 23% of them responded to Direct Mail.

- 33% will open direct mail that is deemed to contain relevant information.

25 – 34

- 43% of them responded to Direct Mail.

- 73% will open direct mail that is deemed to contain relevant information.

35 – 44

- 46% of them responded to Direct Mail.

- 1.5 Million of them visited a shop as a result of Direct Mail.

45 – 54

- 47% of them responded to Direct Mail.

- 25% more likely to open Direct Mail compared to other age groups

55 – 64

- **79% of them responded to Direct Mail.**

- **1.5 Million of them responded to a money off voucher.**

65+

- **92% of them responded to Direct Mail.**

- **6.1 Million of them ordered something seen on a Direct Mail piece.**

I'd like to draw your attention to the last two age groups marked in bold. Have you noticed how tremendously high these two groups' response rate to direct mail is? I think the lesson to be learned from this is that if you are targeting customers between the age group of 55 to 65+ for your company, the only form of marketing you should be using is direct mail marketing.

Why?

Because no other method will give you a response rate of 80% -92%.

In closing;

First of all, I'd like to congratulate you for reading this book to this point.

Throughout the book, I have strived to give you specific tactics and strategies that will help you

- ➤ Increase Your Sales
- ➤ Automate Your Marketing
- ➤ And Dominate Your Niche

In the shortest amount of time, if you follow the instructions given, take the bull by the horn, take accountability and most importantly take massive (planned) action.

These are not some theoretical text book strategies, these are the strategies we use every day to grow our businesses and help all of our clients do the same. We are in trenches everyday just like you are and understand what you go through every day.

You have a product/service/practice, you are passionate about and you'd like to maximize your efforts, income and ROI by using the best tools. And in this books I have tried to present you those best tools.

These words are not coming from an "Online Guru" sitting on top of a proverbial mountain totally disconnected from the realities of start-ups and small businesses, and try to pull you into his/her bubble of "get rich quick" schemes.

Years of experience, countless hours of reading, studying, applying and measuring goes into the practice of the strategies taught in this book.

Here is a recap

With the 7 time tested and proven strategies for your Start up or Small Business.

You have learned

-How to Attract Qualified Leads to Your Website

-How not to make the most common website design mistakes.

-Understand and use the massive power of Social Media

-Follow up with the prospects who didn't buy the first time and automate the process

-How to use Multi-Channel Marketing principles to dominate your niche.

-How to maximize the impact of online reviews to your benefit.

-How do dominate the search engines in the shortest amount of time

-How to use the proven power of Direct Mail Marketing to your advantage for the first time at massive scale.

I congratulate you taking action for your business. I am looking forward to hearing your success stories. Don't hesitate to hit me up with e mails or calls to ask questions or share your take aways from this book. It truly means a lot to me.

Cheers

To your success.

About the Author;

Oguz Konar became the CEO of his first company at age 28. He has seven years of online and offline sales management and marketing experience. After witnessing his family's small business fall apart due to financial and marketing illiteracy, he decided to take action and learn the secrets of sales and marketing to keep other small business owners from making the same mistakes.

He is the creator of a proven system called **_Direct Mail Marketing Machine_** which is a DONE-FOR-YOU direct mailing system for busy professionals who needs predictable flow of new business now. This proven system helped Oguz Konar receive the honorable award of ***The 2014 Product Creator Excellence Award by Make Market Launch IT community***.

He's also the owner and the founder of Local Marketing Stars, where he helps professionals and small business owners attract new clients and grow their business exponentially by becoming the ultimate authority in their field of expertise. As a token of the quality and consistency of Local Marketing Stars, The company has been awarded ***The 2014 3ʳᵈ World Quality Award By Lobin World*** .

He's a strategic marketing consultant on categories such as video marketing, social media marketing, reputation management, lead generation and sales management, market research, business plan preparation.

Oguz published his first book ***"10 Ways to Grow Your Practice In The New Age of Marketing."*** in September 2013 which became the Amazon bestselling book within the first month of publishing.

He's the founder of 4 companies that he's currently running and he spends most of his time consulting his clients on implementing effective, productive and no-nonsense marketing strategies to maximize their income in the shortest amount of time.
He's a non-fiction book worm, loves fishing and traveling.
He can be reached at info@localmarketingstars.com

Or at www.localmarketingstars.com

Oguz Konar

THANK YOU

LOCAL MARKETING STARS

54 WEST 40TH ST.

NEW YORK, NY 10018

info@localmarketingstars.com

www.localmarketingstars.com

www.ingramcontent.com/pod-product-compliance
Lightning Source LLC
Chambersburg PA
CBHW070808180526
45168CB00002B/541